The Hydrogen Bomb

& _{even} More **Yo-Yo** Stuff

by **Richie**

published by **Butterfingers**

The Blurb

The Hydrogen Bomb & Even More Yo-Yo Stuff
by Richie
Copyright © R.D.Windsor 1998
All rights reserved.

First edition
Published by Butterfingers, Bristol.

ISBN 1-898591-17-2

Illustrations by "Mark"
Layout & Design by Charlie Dancey.
Printed by Devenish & Co. Bath.

The Hydrogen Bomb

Welcome to the Hydrogen Bomb (and Even More Yo-Yo Stuff), the second in this series of yo-yo books, the first being Splitting the Atom and Other Yo-Yo Stuff which covered some basics in yo-yo play. Since I wrote Splitting the Atom a year ago I have learned a lot more, much of which is within these pages.

Some of the tricks here are fairly simple, some are slightly more challenging and some are downright difficult. But hey! Just like anything in life, if you want to do something badly enough then you can do it. With practice and dedication, anything is possible.

All I hope is that everyone who buys this book learns at least a few new tricks to add to their repertoire.

Only then will I feel that I have done my job as an author and a source of information.

RICHIE

CONTENTS

Throughout this book you'll see tricks explained in terms of other tricks. For example, if you want to learn the **BANK DEPOSIT** you'll need to throw a **SLEEPER**.

To make it easy I've put all these trick references in **BOLD TYPE**.

If you can't find one of these tricks in this book, then you'll find it in "Splitting the Atom".

Of course if you don't have "Splitting the Atom" you have a problem because these two books go together like **CHEESE AND ONION**.

CONTENTS

A LITTLE MORE ON STRINGING YOUR YO-YO

IN SPLITTING THE ATOM I SPOKE A LITTLE ABOUT SINGLE AND DOUBLE LOOPING BUT WHAT I DIDN'T EXPLAIN WAS HOW TO DO IT AND WHAT EFFECT IT HAS SO I'M GOING TO PUT THAT RIGHT NOW.

I THINK THE DIAGRAM IS FAIRLY SELF-EXPLANATORY.

SINGLE **DOUBLE** **TRIPLE**

PUTTING ON THE FIRST LOOP

...AND THE SECOND

SOME YO-YOS MAY EVEN REQUIRE A THIRD LOOP (TRIPLE LOOPING). AS A RULE YOU SHOULD ONLY USE DOUBLE OR TRIPLE LOOPS ON A TRANSAXLE YO-YO. THE MORE LOOPS YOU USE, THE MORE RESPONSIVE YOUR YO-YO WILL BE, BUT AT THE EXPENSE OF SMOOTH PLAY DURING STRING TRICKS.

YOU SHOULD EXPERIMENT WITH DIFFERENT NUMBERS OF LOOPS TO FIND WHAT SUITS YOU AND YOUR YO-YO BEST.

THUMB WIND
FROM A DEAD YO-YO, USE THE THUMB OF YOUR FREE HAND TO START THE YO-YO SPINNING. IT HELPS TO FEED THE STRING IN TO THE YO-YO WITH YOUR YO-HAND. PRACTICE THIS EVERY TIME YOUR YO-YO DIES AND VERY SOON YOU WILL HAVE THIS ONE DONE AND DUSTED.

FOOT POP WIND

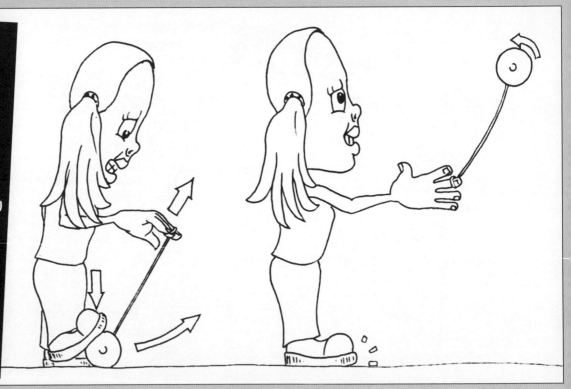

FOOT POP WIND

HAVE THE YO-YO ON THE FLOOR IN FRONT OF YOU.

PLACE YOUR FOOT ON THE YO-YO AND PUSH DOWN.

THE YO-YO WILL POP OUT IN FRONT OF YOU AND WIND BACK UP THE STRING.

CAUTION: THIS CAN DAMAGE YOUR YO-YO!

BUT HEY! IT LOOKS COOL WHEN IT WORKS...

The Hydrogen Bomb

WRONG WAY WIND

START TO WIND THE STRING AROUND THE YO-YO THE WRONG WAY FOR 2 OR 3 WRAPS.

THEN WIND THE REMAINDER IN THE GROOVE.

YOU SHOULD END UP WITH SOMETHING THAT RESEMBLES A PARCEL.

THROW DOWN AS NORMAL...

YO FACTS: THE **YO-YO** IS THOUGHT TO BE THE SECOND OLDEST TOY... THE **DOLL** BEING THE OLDEST.

SNAP

HOLD THE YO-YO BETWEEN THE THUMB AND YO FINGER OF YOUR YO-HAND.

FLICK THE YO-YO TO START IT SPINNING.

THE ACTION IS SIMILAR TO SNAPPING YOUR FINGERS.

WITH PRACTICE YOU CAN GET THE YO-YO TO WIND UP COMPLETELY WITH JUST ONE SNAP OF YOUR FINGERS.

MOON LANDING

FROM **REACH FOR THE MOON**, SIMPLY INTERCEPT THE STRING WITH YOUR THUMB ON THE UP STROKE AS THE YO-YO RETURNS.

TRY TO CATCH IT ON THE CRADLE BETWEEN YOUR THUMB AND FOREFINGER.

HOW COOL IS THIS TRICK?

ROLL BACK OVER YOUR THUMB AND OUT TO FINISH.

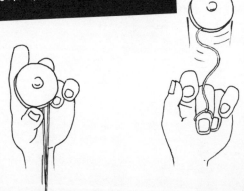

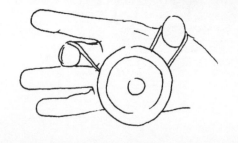

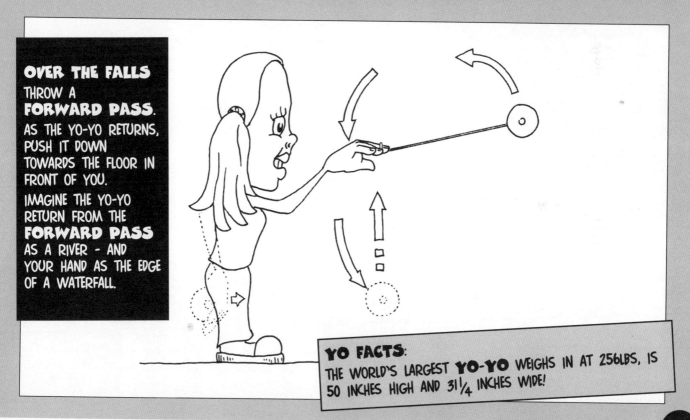

OVER THE FALLS

THROW A **FORWARD PASS**.

AS THE YO-YO RETURNS, PUSH IT DOWN TOWARDS THE FLOOR IN FRONT OF YOU.

IMAGINE THE YO-YO RETURN FROM THE **FORWARD PASS** AS A RIVER - AND YOUR HAND AS THE EDGE OF A WATERFALL.

YO FACTS:
THE WORLD'S LARGEST **YO-YO** WEIGHS IN AT 256LBS, IS 50 INCHES HIGH AND 31¼ INCHES WIDE!

SIX SHOOTER   IMPOSSIBLE ROLLER COASTER

SIX SHOOTER

THROW A **SLEEPER** AND GO INTO A STRING MOUNT, AS IN THE **BRAIN TWISTER**.

TRANSFER THE LOOP OF STRING FROM YOUR FREE HAND TO YOUR YO-FINGER. NOW SWING THE YO-YO AROUND YOUR YO-FINGER IN A MINI-**AROUND THE WORLD** TYPE MOTION.

(THE STRING WILL START TO WIND AROUND YOUR FINGER AFTER 2 OR 3 REVOLUTIONS)

STRAIGHTEN YOUR FINGER AND LET THE YO-YO FLY FORWARDS AS IN A **FORWARD PASS**

IMPOSSIBLE ROLLER COASTER

THE SAME AS A **SIX SHOOTER** EXCEPT YOU CONTINUE TO CIRCLE THE YO-YO AROUND YOUR FINGER UNTIL THE STRING IS USED UP AND THE YO-YO JAMS AGAINST YOUR FINGER. THEN REVERSE THE MANOEUVRE, CAUSING THE STRING TO WIND BACK AROUND THE YO-YO. FLICK THE YO-YO FORWARDS AND OFF YOUR FINGER JUST AS THE STRING IS ALL USED UP. NOT EASY BUT VERY COOL WHEN IT WORKS OUT.

ATOMIC DRED'S HOT TIPS

PENDULUM

TRAPEZE COMBO

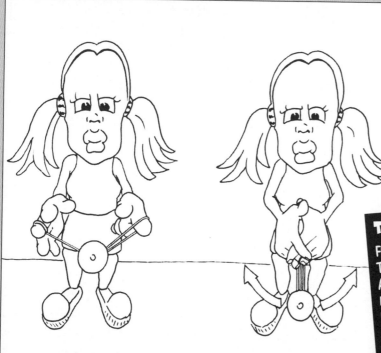

PENDULUM

THROW A **TRAPEZE** BRING YOUR HANDS TOGETHER AND SWING THE YO-YO FROM SIDE TO SIDE LIKE THE PENDULUM OF A CLOCK.

ALSO CALLED THE "MAN ON THE FLYING TRAPEZE" THIS SIMPLE TRICK LOOKS VERY EFFECTIVE IN A SERIES OF TRAPEZE MOUNTS.

TRAPEZE COMBO

FROM A **TRAPEZE**, THROW THE YO-YO OFF TO THE SIDE OVER YOUR FREE HAND AND AROUND INTO **DOUBLE OR NOTHING**. HOLD FOR A FEW SECONDS AND REVERSE BACK INTO A **TRAPEZE** FINISH WITH A FLASHY DISMOUNT.

ATOMIC DRED'S HOT TIPS

BABY FACE

FROM A **SLEEPER** - DRAPE THE STRING AROUND YOUR NECK, PINCH THE STRING AND LEAN BACKWARDS.

NOW ROCK THE BABY ABOVE YOUR FACE.

WARNING!

THIS IS A POTENTIALLY DANGEROUS TRICK.

ONLY ATTEMPT IT WHEN YOU ARE REALLY CONFIDENT WITH A YO-YO.

DON'T SAY I DIDN'T WARN YOU!!!

EXTRA POINTS...

FINISH BY DROPPING BACK DOWN TO A **GUILLOTINE** FINISH.

YO FACTS: IN **FRANCE** DURING THE 1700'S THE **YO-YO** WAS KNOWN AS THE **BANDALORE**.

DOG BITE

THROW A GOOD **SLEEPER** AND ALLOW THE YO-YO TO SWING THROUGH YOUR LEGS.

AS IT MAKES CONTACT WITH YOUR TROUSERS A TUG ON THE STRING SHOULD CAUSE THE YO-YO TO **BITE** ONTO THE MATERIAL.

SHOW YOUR AUDIENCE AND TUG THE STRING TO LOOSEN DOGGY'S GRIP AND RETURN TO YOUR HAND.

BANK DEPOSIT

BANK DEPOSIT

THROW A **SLEEPER** MORE OUT THAN DOWN.

ALLOW IT TO SWING THROUGH YOUR LEGS, AROUND YOUR THIGH AND INTO YOUR POCKET.

HOW COOL A FINISH IS THIS?

VERY COOL INDEED!!

TRY **BANK DEPOSIT** FROM ANY TRICK THAT ENDS WITH A "ROLL OUT DISMOUNT", SUCH AS THE **BRAIN TWISTER** OR **SPLITTING THE ATOM**.

A "ROLL OUT DISMOUNT" IS THE SECOND HALF OF THE **BRAIN TWISTER**

BIRD IN THE HAND

GO INTO **AROUND THE WORLD** FROM A **BREAKAWAY**, LET THE STRING WRAP AROUND YOUR FOREFINGER AND YO-FINGER.

AT THE LAST MINUTE, POP OUT YOUR THUMB TO INTERCEPT THE STRING, CAUSING THE YO-YO TO HOP ONTO THE CRADLE YOU HAVE JUST MADE.

IT HELPS TO COUNT THE NUMBER OF WRAPS AROUND YOUR FINGERS - ADJUST AS NEEDED

YO FACTS:
THE WORD **YO-YO** ORIGINATES FROM THE PHILIPINO WORD "TAGALOG" MEANING "COME COME".

THROUGH THE SUBWAY

THROUGH THE SUBWAY

THROW A REVERSE **AROUND THE WORLD** (RETRO). AS IT COMPLETES THE CIRCUIT, LET THE YO-YO DOWN TO THE FLOOR AND BEND YOUR BODY FORWARDS AS YOU DO SO. SWING THE YO-YO THROUGH YOUR LEGS AS FAR AS IT WILL GO BEFORE RETURNING THE YO-YO AS IN THE **CREEPER**.

TRY THIS:

THIS IS ALSO POSSIBLE FROM A NORMAL **AROUND THE WORLD**, LETTING THE YO-YO DOWN IN FRONT OF YOU AND WALKING IT BACKWARDS THROUGH YOUR LEGS TO A **CREEPER**.

TURBO SUBWAY

THROW A DOUBLE **ROUND THE WORLD** - AS IT REACHES 360 DEGREES, TURN YOUR BODY 180 DEGREES. WITH YOUR LEGS APART, ALLOW THE YO-YO TO GO THROUGH AND EXECUTE A **CREEPER**.

HAVING CAUGHT THE YO-YO AT GROUND LEVEL YOU CAN GO STRAIGHT INTO A DOUBLE **AROUND THE WORLD** AND REPEAT THE WHOLE TRICK AGAIN.

JOHNNY ROUND THE CORNER

THROW AN **AROUND THE WORLD** AND LET THE YO-YO COME AROUND AND UNDER YOUR ARM, THEN INTERCEPT THE STRING WITH YOUR FREE HAND'S FOREFINGER AND THE YO-YO WILL HOP OVER AND LAND ON THE STRING (RATHER LIKE A **TRAPEZE**).

SIMPLY REVERSE TO FINISH.

AROUND THE BLOCK

AROUND THE BLOCK

THROW THE YO-YO DOWN AND ACROSS YOUR BODY (SIMILAR TO A **FLYING SAUCER** OR **UFO**).

LET THE YO-YO TOUCH DOWN ON THE FLOOR AS FAR BEHIND YOU AS POSSIBLE.

WALK IT IN A CIRCLE AROUND YOU.

FOR EXTRA POINTS, THROW A LOOP AS IT RETURNS.

TEXAS COWBOY

HOLD THE YO-YO SIDEWAYS AND THROW A HORIZONTAL **AROUND THE WORLD** ABOVE YOUR HEAD. AS GRAVITY TAKES EFFECT AND THE YO-YO DROPS, EITHER STEP OR JUMP OVER THE STRING BEFORE RETURNING THE YO-YO TO YOUR HAND.

REGENERATION

REGENERATING THE SPIN OF THE YO-YO WHEN IT HAS SLOWED DOWN IS A USEFUL AND IMPORTANT PART OF FREESTYLE YO-YO PLAY. IT CAN BE DONE FROM JUST ABOUT ANY TRICK. **WARP DRIVE** IS A GOOD EXAMPLE OF REGENERATION AS IS **TIME WARP**.

REGENERATION OF A **FORWARD PASS** IS A GOOD PLACE TO START.

AS THE YO-YO RETURNS FROM A FORWARD PASS, WHIP YOUR HAND AROUND THE TOP OF THE YO-YO, PUSHING IT DOWN INTO A **SLEEPER**.

APPLY THIS PRINCIPLE TO ANY RETURNING YO-YO FROM ANY ANGLE AND YOU CAN KEEP THE YO-YO SPINNING INDEFINITELY (IN THEORY) ALTHOUGH 2 TO 3 MINUTES IS GOOD IN PRACTICE.

DR. WHO

FORWARD PASS INTO SEVEN REGENERATIONS OF SPIN...

HOW MANY REGENERATIONS DID DR. WHO HAVE?

TIME WARP

THROW AN **AROUND THE WORLD** AND AS IT RETURNS, WHIP AROUND THE YO-YO TO REGENERATE THE SPIN AND GO STRAIGHT INTO A RETRO (REVERSE) **AROUND THE WORLD.**

COMET

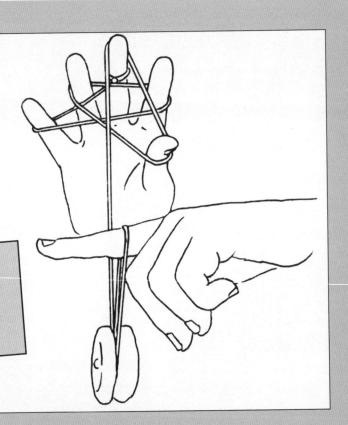

YO FACTS:
THE LONGEST **SLEEPER** RECORD FOR A FIXED AXLE IS 57 SECONDS. THE LONGEST SLEEPER FOR A TRANSAXLE? MY PERSONAL BEST FOR WHAT IT'S WORTH IS 3 MINUTES 40 SECONDS TO EXTINCTION - **BEAT THAT!**

IN THE BUCKET

THROW A **SLEEPER** OUT TO YOUR SIDE AND DRAPE THE STRING OVER THE PALM OF YOUR FREE HAND BETWEEN THE THUMB AND FOREFINGER

NOW WRAP THE STRING AROUND YOUR THUMB AND FOREFINGER

WITH YOUR YO-HAND, PICK UP THE STRING THAT RUNS FROM YOUR FREE HAND THUMB OVER THE BACK OF THE HAND TO FORM THE BUCKET.

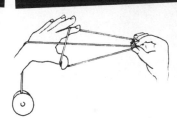

FLIP THE YO-YO OVER YOUR FREE HAND AND INTO THE BUCKET, CATCHING IT ON THE MIDDLE STRING

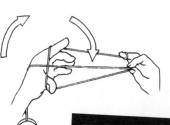

REVERSE TO FINISH...

BUCKET TO TRAPEZE

THROW THE YO-YO BACK OUT OF THE BUCKET AND AROUND INTO A **TRAPEZE**.

MAGIC

THROW A **SLEEPER** AND DRAPE THE STRING OVER THE BACK OF YOUR FREE HAND WITH ALL YOUR FINGERS SPREAD.

1

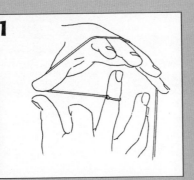

2

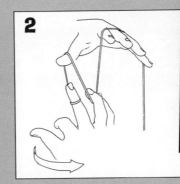

NOW USING THE THIRD FINGER OF YOUR YO-HAND, PULL THE STRING BETWEEN THE THUMB AND FOREFINGER OF YOUR FREE HAND RATHER LIKE A MINI REVERSE **DRAWBACK**.

3

4

TWIST YOUR YO-HAND WRIST TO MAKE A LOOP, AND THEN TRANSFER THE LOOP ONTO THE FOREFINGER OF YOUR FREE HAND.

NOW DO THE SAME WITH THE STRING BETWEEN THE FORE AND MIDDLE FINGER OF YOUR FREE HAND PLACING THE LOOP ONTO THE MIDDLE FINGER AND CONTINUE ALL THE WAY ALONG THE FINGERS OF YOUR FREE HAND.

5

YO FACTS: THE **YO-YO** IS THOUGHT TO DATE BACK TO 500BC, ORIGINATING IN **CHINA**

6

FINALLY, DROP THE LOOP OFF THE THUMB OF YOUR FREE HAND AND PULL YOUR YO-HAND AWAY FROM YOU.

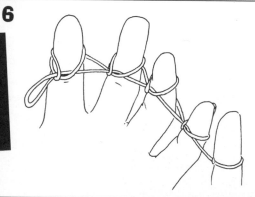

IF YOU HAVE DONE IT RIGHT THEN ALL THE LOOPS SHOULD JUST FALL AWAY...

LIKE MAGIC!

ROCK THE BABY UNDER THE EIFFEL TOWER

FROM A **TRAPEZE** BRING THE STRING OVER THE FOREFINGER OF YOUR FREE HAND.

NOW, WITH THE FOREFINGER OF YOUR YO-HAND, PICK UP THE EXTRA STRING YOU HAVE CREATED - AT THE SAME TIME PLACE THE THUMB OF YOUR FREE HAND IN THE LOOP ALONGSIDE THE FOREFINGER.

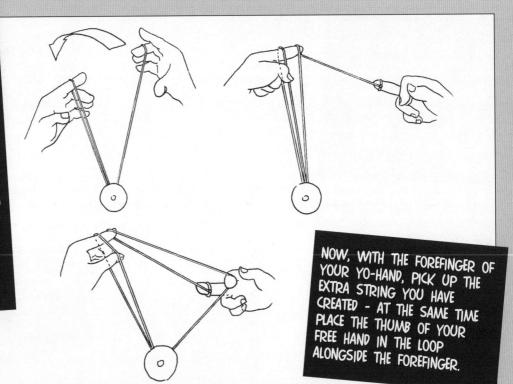

NOW, WITH THE FOREFINGER OF YOUR YO-HAND, PICK UP THE EXTRA STRING YOU HAVE CREATED - AT THE SAME TIME PLACE THE THUMB OF YOUR FREE HAND IN THE LOOP ALONGSIDE THE FOREFINGER.

...ROCK THE BABY UNDER THE EIFFEL TOWER

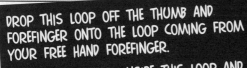

DROP THIS LOOP OFF THE THUMB AND FOREFINGER ONTO THE LOOP COMING FROM YOUR FREE HAND FOREFINGER.

PLACE YOUR THUMB INSIDE THIS LOOP AND OPEN UP TO FORM THE CRADLE.

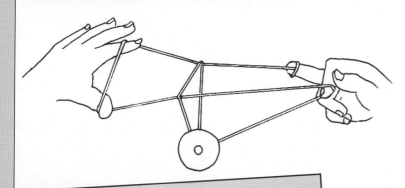

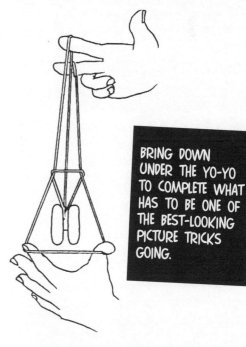

BRING DOWN UNDER THE YO-YO TO COMPLETE WHAT HAS TO BE ONE OF THE BEST-LOOKING PICTURE TRICKS GOING.

YO FACTS:
THE FIRST **SLEEPING** YO-YO'S WERE INTRODUCED BY **PEDRO FLORES** IN THE 1920'S

TWO'S COMPANY

TWO-HANDED LOOPS

TWO-HANDED YO-YO PLAY IS VERY IMPRESSIVE TO WATCH, CHALLENGING TO LEARN, AND FEELS SO GOOD WHEN YOU FINALLY GET IT RIGHT.

THE FIRST THING TO DO IS TO WORK WITH YOUR WEAKER HAND.

PRACTICE **LOOPS** AND **HOP THE FENCE** TO START WITH AS A LOT OF TWO-HANDED YO-YO PLAY IS BASED AROUND THESE TWO TRICKS.

ONCE YOU FEEL THAT YOU ARE READY TO GO FOR TWO YO-YO'S AT THE SAME TIME, START WITH ALTERNATING THROW DOWN AND **FORWARD PASS** THROWS AND BUILD UP TO **LOOPS**, **AROUND THE WORLDS** AND **REACH FOR THE MOONS** - AND WHATEVER ELSE YOU FANCY.

THE SKY'S THE LIMIT!

TWO HANDED LOOPS

LOOPING THE LOOP WITH BOTH HANDS ALTERNATING IS A LOT EASIER THAN TRYING TO DO IT IN SYNC.

FEEL FREE TO TRY BOTH METHODS!

YO FACTS:
THE FIRST **YO-YO** PLAYER IN **SPACE** WAS **DAVID GRIGGS** IN 1984 AS PART OF THE **NASA** TOYS IN SPACE PROJECT.

CRISS CROSS

MILK THE COW

CRISS CROSS

START LOOPING WITH BOTH HANDS AND SLOWLY START TO CROSS THEM IN FRONT OF YOU.

IT HELPS TO SLIGHTLY MOVE YOUR ELBOWS OUT FROM YOUR BODY.

MILK THE COW

ALTERNATING REVERSE LOOPS (**HOP THE FENCE**) WITH BOTH HANDS.

PRACTICE WITH EACH HAND SEPARATELY, AND THEN GO FOR IT.

WHEN YOU GET THIS ONE DOWN IT SHOULD LOOK LIKE YOU ARE MILKING A COW.

IF YOU HAVE NEVER MILKED A COW YOU WILL JUST HAVE TO USE YOUR IMAGINATION - LIKE I DID!!

PUNCHING BAG

PUNCHING BAG

THROW LOOPS WITH ONE HAND AND REVERSE LOOPS (HOP THE FENCE) WITH THE OTHER.

THE REVERSE LOOPS SHOULD BE THROWN HORIZONTALLY OUT IN FRONT OF YOU.

PRACTICE THROWING **HOP THE FENCE**, AND SLOWLY BRING IT UP TO THE HORIZONTAL POSITION.

ATOMIC DRED'S HOT TIPS

RIDE THE HORSE

PRACTICE REVERSE LOOPS TO THE SIDE AND BACK OF YOU. THIS FORMS THE BACK OF THE HORSE. ONCE YOU HAVE MASTERED THIS, ADD **LOOP THE LOOP** WITH THE OTHER HAND TO FORM THE FRONT OF THE HORSE.

BOB YOUR BODY UP AND DOWN A LITTLE AS YOU PERFORM THIS FOR ADDED EFFECT.

WATCH THE REVERSE LOOP RATHER THAN THE FORWARD LOOP THE LOOP.

SAYING THINGS LIKE "RIDE 'EM COWBOY!" ISN'T FUNNY - BUT IT MIGHT HELP!

SHOOT THE MOON

SHOOT THE MOON

LOOP THE LOOP WITH ONE HAND AND **REACH FOR THE MOON** WITH THE OTHER.

CONCENTRATE ON THE REACH FOR THE MOON.

THIS IS A HARD ONE BUT WELL WORTH THE EFFORT.

STICK WITH IT!

YO FACTS: A GOOD QUALITY **YO-YO** IS CAPABLE OF SPIN SPEEDS IN EXCESS OF 11,000 RPM,!!

STRICTLY SPEAKING (AND DESPITE WHAT I SAID IN "SPLITTING THE ATOM") **REACH FOR THE MOON** IS THE RIGHT NAME FOR THE ONE-HANDED TRICK AND **SHOOT THE MOON** IS THIS ONE!

SO NOW YOU KNOW!!

TWO-HANDED REACH FOR THE MOON

TWO-HANDED REACH FOR THE MOON

AS YOU WOULD IMAGINE, YOU **REACH FOR THE MOON** WITH BOTH HANDS AT THE SAME TIME.

THIS HAS TO BE THE HARDEST TWO-HANDED TRICK THERE IS.

PRACTICE WITH YOUR WEAKER HAND A LOT BEFORE YOU ATTEMPT IT WITH BOTH.

IF YOU GET THIS ONE THEN YOU ARE A TRUE YO-YO **MASTER!**

PUT MORE ENERGY INTO THE OUT THROWS AND TRY TO KEEP THEM AT ABOUT 45° TO THE HORIZONTAL.

LOCK YOUR WRIST AS THEY RETURN FOR THE UP STROKES.

TRY TO KEEP THE STRING FEEDING IN AND OUT OF THE GROOVE.

ATOMIC DRED'S HOT TIPS

THE HYDROGEN BOMB...

THE HYDROGEN BOMB

START WITH A **TRAPEZE** THROW BUT MISS! - LETTING THE YO-YO PASS BETWEEN THE STRING AND YOUR BODY.

TURN YOUR BODY TOWARDS YOUR FREE HAND AND USE THE FOREFINGER OF YOUR YO-HAND TO INTERCEPT THE STRING A FEW INCHES ABOVE THE YO-YO.

CATCH THE YO-YO ON THE STRING!

YOU SHOULD NOW BE IN A POSITION JUST LIKE THE FIRST STAGE OF **SPLITTING THE ATOM** ONLY BACKWARDS!

(SEE PAGE 39 OF **SPLITTING THE ATOM**)

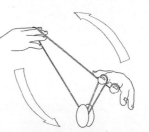

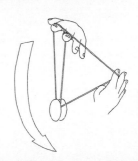

NOW BRING YOUR FREE HAND UNDER THE YO-YO FOLLOWED BY YOUR YO-HAND AND CONTINUE THIS REVERSE CYCLING MOTION (**BARREL ROLLS**) FOR A FEW CIRCUITS.

YOU MUST FINISH THIS SEQUENCE WITH TWO FREE HAND UNDER PASSES, CATCHING THE YO-YO ON THE DOUBLE STRINGS*.

DROP THE LOOP OFF THE YO-HAND FINGER AND YOU SHOULD BE IN A DOUBLED **TRAPEZE** POSITION.

PULL YOUR FREE HAND UPWARDS AND YOUR YO-HAND DOWNWARDS FOR A SPECTACULAR FINISH

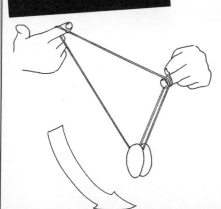

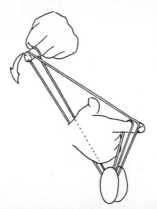

*IN ANOTHER VERSION, THE YO-YO IS CAUGHT ONLY ON THE INSIDE STRING. (THE REST OF THE TRICK STAYS THE SAME).

IT'S HARDER TO DO, BUT IT DOESN'T SLOW THE YO-YO DOWN SO MUCH.

CHEESE AND ONION

CHEESE AND ONION

THIS OUTRAGEOUSLY DIFFICULT COMBINATION TRICK WAS THOUGHT UP BY ANTON MACMAN. PRACTICE EACH TRICK SEPARATELY AND THEN LINK THEM ALL TOGETHER.

THROW A FAST **SLEEPER**.

EXECUTE A **PULLOVER**, CATCHING THE YO-YO ON THE STRING.

BY RAISING YOUR YO-HAND AND LOWERING THE OTHER THE YO-YO WILL SHOOT OUT IN FRONT OF YOU.

PLACE THE FINGER OF YOUR FREE HAND MIDWAY ON THE STRING AND EXECUTE A SPLIT BOTTOM MOUNT...

CONTINUE INTO **SPLITTING THE ATOM** WITH A DOUBLE OUT AND **PINWHEEL**.

EXECUTE A **REGENERATION**.

CONTINUE INTO THE **HYDROGEN BOMB** WITH A DOUBLE OUT.

EXECUTE A **REGENERATION**.

CONTINUE INTO **TRAPEZE COMBO**.

FINISH BY CATCHING THE YO-YO BETWEEN THE MIDDLE AND FOREFINGER OF YOUR YO-HAND - **OR**...

(THIS IS MY LITTLE ADDITION)

GO INTO **REACH FOR THE MOON** AND FINISH WITH A **MOON LANDING**.

THE WRITING OF THIS BOOK HAS BEEN HARD WORK AND GOOD FUN ALL AT THE SAME TIME AND IT HAS ONLY BEEN MADE POSSIBLE WITH THE HELP AND INSPIRATION OF SOME PEOPLE WHO DESERVE BIG RESPECT.

JACKIE, **JOSH**, **JAKE**, **ISAAC** AND **LOUIS** FOR PUTTING UP WITH ME AND **MARK** FOR HIS FANTASTIC ARTWORK.

BEN, **HANS**, **JAMES**, **HOWIE**, **MATT**, **REV**, **TIM** AND THE **AIRTIME YO-YO** TEAM FOR INSPIRATION. **LAURIE**, **PAUL** AND **RICK** FOR BELIEVING IN ME, **CHARLIE** FOR LAYING IT OUT, AND EVERYONE ELSE WHO HAS MADE THIS BOOK POSSIBLE.

BUT MOST OF ALL I WOULD LIKE TO THANK THE PERSON WHO INVENTED THE FIRST YO-YO FOR HAVING SUCH A FANTASTIC IDEA.

I THINK MY FINAL WORDS IN THIS BOOK ARE FOR EVERYONE WHO READS IT AND THOSE WORDS ARE **PRACTICE PRACTICE PRACTICE** AND WHEN YOU HAVE FINISHED THAT **PRACTICE** SOME MORE.

RICHIE

YO FACTS:
GOD CREATED THE WORLD IN 6 DAYS AND ON THE 7TH HE PLAYED WITH A **YO-YO** (NOT REALLY TRUE BUT A NICE THOUGHT)

ABOUT THE AUTHOR

RICHIE WINDSOR (STILL NO RELATION) IS 35 NOW. HE LEARNT TO JUGGLE AT THE AGE OF 18. BY THE AGE OF 20, HE HAD GIVEN UP HIS JOB AS A PAINTER AND DECORATOR AND WAS EARNING HIS LIVING AS A PROFESSIONAL JUGGLER, WORKING ALL OVER THE WORLD.

IN THE PAST 15 YEARS HE HAS VISITED MOST OF EUROPE, WORKING ON STREET, SCREEN AND STAGE. SOME OF THE MORE MEMORABLE INCLUDE A HYDRAULIC STAGE IN MALTA, AND A THEATRE IN SARAJEVO, BOSNIA, DURING THE WAR.

HE TAKES A BROAD VIEW OF JUGGLING AND SEES IT AS OBJECT MANIPULATION AND IS STILL AMAZED AT WHAT CAN BE ACHIEVED THROUGH REPETITIVE PRACTICE AND SHEER DETERMINATION IN SEARCH OF PERFECTION.

RICHIE BECAME INTERESTED IN THE YO-YO FOUR YEARS AGO WHEN HE TOOK OVER A SMALL MARKET STALL, SELLING JUGGLING EQUIPMENT. THAT DEVELOPED INTO "AIRTIME" - EXETER BASED SPECIALISTS IN OBJECTS THAT REQUIRE HUMAN INTERACTION AND ENDEAVOUR SUCH AS - JUGGLING EQUIPMENT, KITES, BOOMERANGS AND YO-YOS.

THIS LED HIM TO WRITE **SPLITTING THE ATOM** WHICH MUST BE JUST ABOUT THE BESTSELLING YO-YO BOOK EVER WRITTEN. HAVING DECIDED THAT YOU CAN'T HAVE TOO MUCH OF A GOOD THING HE SAT DOWN AND WROTE THIS BOOK AS WELL. PERHAPS THERE WILL BE MORE?

FINALLY, THE FIVE MOST IMPORTANT PEOPLE IN HIS LIFE ARE HIS WONDERFULLY TOLERANT AND LOVELY WIFE, JACKIE, AND THEIR FANTASTICALLY NAUGHTY BOYS - JOSH, ISAAC, JAKE AND LOUIS.